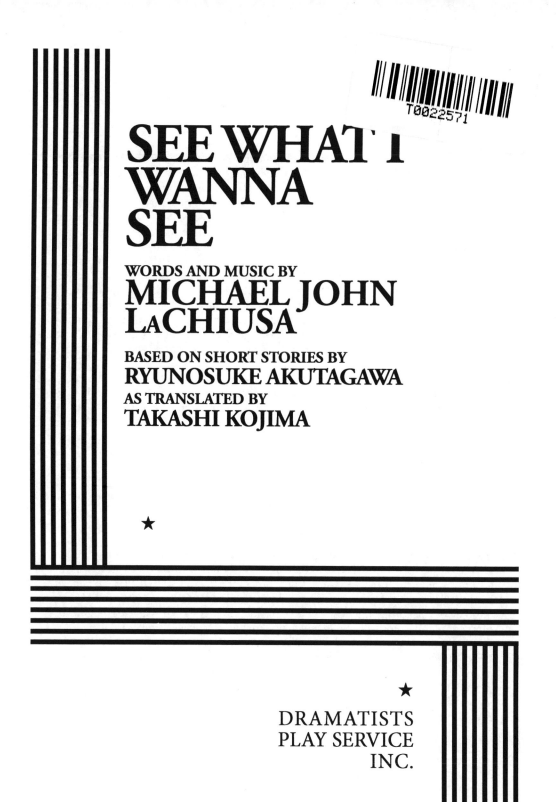

SEE WHAT I WANNA SEE

WORDS AND MUSIC BY
MICHAEL JOHN LaCHIUSA

BASED ON SHORT STORIES BY
RYUNOSUKE AKUTAGAWA

AS TRANSLATED BY
TAKASHI KOJIMA

★

★

DRAMATISTS
PLAY SERVICE
INC.

The following acknowledgment must appear in a clear and prominent position on the title page in all programs distributed in connection with performances of the Play:

Originally produced in October 2005 at the Public Theater,
Oskar Eustis, Artistic Director; Mara Manus, Executive Director.

In addition, the following acknowledgments must appear directly beneath the acknowledgment above in size of type not less than 35% of the size of its largest, most prominent letter:

The World Premiere of SEE WHAT I WANNA SEE
was produced by the Williamstown Theatre Festival,
Michael Ritchie, Producer.

SEE WHAT I WANNA SEE was commissioned by and developed at
Musical Theatre Works, Thomas Cott, Artistic Director,
with the generous support of the
Gilman Gonzalez-Falla Foundation
and Ted and Mary Jo Shen and the Shen Family Foundation.

For Wiley, with thanks

SET DESIGN AND COSTUME NOTES

The set design for SEE WHAT I WANNA SEE must be minimalist. A bare stage is preferable — a raised platform, slightly raked. There should be a nod to the Japanese roots of these stories, but only in the aesthetic, not cosmetic, sense.

KESA AND MORITO — a long, flowing silk drape should extend across the entire stage — like a Kabuki *hikimaku,* acting as a curtain; reversing itself for the second part, Morito's soliloquy. The costumes for Kesa and Morito should reflect the story's setting: medieval Japan.

R SHOMON — a metal interrogation table, as in a police station, and two utilitarian chairs. A hanging lamp. The table should function much like a *hanamichi.*

GLORYDAY — two simple chairs, like those seen in a church rectory office. A small area of marsh reeds to indicate the park.

Orchestra should be in view, raised above and behind the action.

SEE WHAT I WANNA SEE was presented by the Public Theater (Oskar Eustis, Artistic Director; Mara Manus, Executive Director) in New York City, opening on October 30, 2005. It was directed by Ted Sperling; the set design was by Thomas Lynch; the costume design was by Elizabeth Caitlin Ward; the lighting design was by Christopher Akerlind; the sound design was by Acme Sound Partners; the musical staging was by Jonathan Butterell; the orchestrations were by Bruce Coughlin; the musical director/conductor was Chris Fenwick; the music coordinator was Seymour Red Press; and the production stage manager was Heather Cousens. The cast was as follows:

KESA, THE WIFE and AN ACTRESS .... Idina Menzel
MORITO, THE HUSBAND and A CPA .... Marc Kudisch
THE THIEF and A REPORTER .... Aaron Lohr
THE JANITOR and A PRIEST .... Henry Stram
THE MEDIUM and AUNT MONICA .... Mary Testa

CHARACTERS

KESA AND MORITO:
    KESA
    MORITO

R SHOMON:
    THE JANITOR
    THE THIEF
    THE WIFE
    THE HUSBAND
    THE MEDIUM

GLORYDAY:
    THE PRIEST
    AUNT MONICA
    A CPA
    AN ACTRESS
    A REPORTER

SETTING

KESA AND MORITO is set in medieval Japan.
R SHOMON is set in 1951, New York City.
GLORYDAY is set in the present, New York City.

ACT ONE

KESA AND MORITO (KESA)
R SHOMON

ACT TWO

KESA AND MORITO (MORITO)
GLORYDAY

SEE WHAT I WANNA SEE

ACT ONE

KESA AND MORITO (KESA)

Kesa's bedroom. Night. Kesa appears. Kesa is a beautiful, sensual monster. Morito appears during her narration. We hear her thoughts; her lover does not.

KESA.
TONIGHT I KISS MY LOVER
FOR THE LAST TIME.
HE COMES FOR ME AT MIDNIGHT;
SLIPPING PAST THE GATE;
FLOATING TO MY BED.
I LET HIS HANDS CARESS ME
FOR THE LAST TIME.
HE KNIFES INTO MY BODY
FORCIBLY AND PROUD.
(MY LOVER IS INCREDIBLY ENDOWED.
THICKER THAN MY HUSBAND.)

AND AS I KISS MY LOVER
FOR THE LAST TIME
THE ROOM DISSOLVES AROUND ME;
I DESERT MY BODY;
ALL OF TIME IS GONE.
DUSK IS DAWN
DAWN IS NOON
LATE IS NOW
NOW IS SOON
THIS IS WHAT IT'S LIKE TO BE GOD.

I WATCH MYSELF OUTSIDE MYSELF
SLEEP AND BREATHE AND WAKE AND SIGH,
LAUGH AND KISS AND FUCK AND LIE —
MY GOD, IT'S HELL TO BE GOD.
WATCHING FROM A DISTANCE,
I NEITHER LAUGH NOR CRY
AS THE FLOODGATES ARE OPENED
AND THE INNOCENT DIE.
A LIE BECOMES THE TRUTH
AND THE TRUTH BECOMES A LIE
LIE …
LIE.

(As Morito appears.)

TONIGHT I KISS MY LOVER
FOR THE LAST TIME.
MY HUSBAND KNOWS OUR SECRET.
I'VE CONFESSED MY GUILT,
I'LL END MY LOVER'S LIFE.

(Morito goes to her; embracers her, enters her.)

AND I'LL RETURN TO MY BODY,
TO MY FOUR-CORNERED ROOM.
WHAT I'VE SET IN MOTION
CANNOT BE REVERSED.
TIME
WILL
RESUME …
TIME …
TIME …
TIME!

(In her lover's embrace, Kesa smiles as she reveals a gleaming, deadly knife. Morito grips her tightly around her throat. At the music's climax, Kesa raises her knife to plunge it into her lover's back. Immediate blackout.)

R SHOMON

1951. New York. A police station. An interrogation room. The Janitor is being interrogated.

THE JANITOR. I told ya. I am a janitor. A janitor. At the movie house. The one they was showing the premiere the night before. Big premiere. Japanese pic. Didn't watch it — if it ain't in English, I figure, hang it, right? Manager was mad at me 'cause one of the letters was missing from the marquee so the title of the movie was all screwed up. Big premiere and bigger mess to clean up afterward. Didn't get out till five. Which makes it Sunday morning. Took my usual short-cut home through the park. I told you.
SO WHATCHA WANT ME TO SAY?
I TOLD YA ALL THAT I KNOW.
I TOLD YA ALL THAT I SEEN.
I ONLY TOLD YA THE TRUTH.
THE PARK.
A SCARF.
A BODY.
THE BLOOD.
I didn't see any knife. His knife, probably … His? I mean whoever did it — with the knife you keep talking about. Which I didn't see.
I ONLY TOLD YA THE TRUTH …
(The Janitor fades into the film noir-esque shadows. The Thief is being interrogated.)

THE THIEF. 1951 will be remembered as the year Jimmy Mako terrorized New York City. Huh? And you caught me. Get your names in the papers …
SO WHATCHA WANT ME TO SAY?
YOU GOT ME. YEAH.
I KILLED HIM.
SO WHATCHA WANT ME TO DO?
WHY LIE NOW?
WHY BOTHER?
I'LL GET THE CHAIR ANYWAY.
THAT'S HOW IT GOES.
BOO-HOO.

WASN'T THE FIRST TIME I KILLED SOMEONE.
WON'T BE THE LAST TIME FOR YOU.
'Cept you do it different. You do it legally.
AIN'T SUCH A BIG DEAL.
IT'S EASY WORK.
MURDER IS WHAT I DO BEST.
WHERE I GREW UP, IT'S SOMETHING YOU LEARN,
LIKE PASSIN' YOUR DRIVER'S TEST.
SO WHATCHA WAITIN' TO HEAR?
THE DETAILS?
YOU GOT IT.
LIKE ALL THE SCREAMS AND THE FEAR?
I KNOW YOU.
YOU LIKE IT.
AIN'T AMERICA A HELLUVA TOWN?
FUNKY-DUNKY THINGS GO DOWN.
THE TRUTH THEN.
AND NOTHIN' BUT …
WHATCHA BEEN ITCHIN' TO HEAR.
WHATCHA BEEN DYIN' TO KNOW.
WHATCHA WANT ME TO SAY …

I wasn't lookin' for it. Was about 10 P.M. Saturday. I'm out on the street just waitin' for nothin' or somethin' to happen, hangin' out by the movie house. Jap pic. Then she comes out of the movies.
WALKIN', SHIFTIN', SHAKIN', OOZIN' BY …
NEVER SEEN HER BEFORE.
TASTY THING.
TWO LONG LEGS
AND A COUPLE OF GRANITE EYES.
PLENTY GOING ON THERE
AND PLENTY WISE.
THEN SHE LOOKED AT ME.
I WAS MINDIN' MY OWN BUSINESS.
SHE LOOKED AT ME
AND I WAS TAKEN BY SURPRISE.
I WAS SCROUNGIN' AROUND FOR A CIGARETTE
WHEN I SMELLED PERFUME
AND I'LL NEVER FORGET
THAT GLANCE SHE THREW

LIKE A NO-WIN BET THAT SAID,
"BABY WANTS TO DANCE TONIGHT,"
PLAIN AS PLAIN COULD BE.
BABY WANTS TO ROCK AND ROLL
AND DO THE DO WITH ME WITH ME WITH ME.
I WAS SOBER ENOUGH —
ENOUGH TO KNOW
WHEN SHE LOOKED AT ME
SHE WAS RARIN' TO GO.

(The Wife has entered, followed by her Husband. The Thief interacts with them, flirting with the Wife. As she strides by the Thief she self-consciously drops her red scarf and slowly bends to retrieve it, giving the Thief a look neither interested nor disinterested. She and the Husband exit.)

BUT WHAT DID SHE DO?
SHE WALKED ON BY.
THE PROPERTY OF ONE OF THOSE
GREASED-DOWN, PINSTRIPED GUYS.
OH, SHE'S GOOD AT TEASIN'
AND TELLIN' LIES.
BUT SHE LOOKED AT ME;
LIKE SHE WAS MINE AND NO ONE ELSE'S.
SHE LOOKED AT ME
AND I'M THE DEVIL IN DISGUISE.
I STOLE HER SOUL
WHEN SHE THREW HER GLANCE;
I SAY SHE HAD NO RIGHT TO SETTIN'
FIRE TO MY PANTS —
MY HEAD WAS ALL A-BUZZIN'
FULL OF ARMY ANTS SCREAMING:
"BABY'S GONNA DANCE, ALL RIGHT."
RIGHT ACROSS THE TAPPANZEE.
GONNA MAKE HER CRY AND BEG
AND DO THE DO WITH ME, WITH ME, WITH ME
IT WAS HER OWN DAMN FAULT
FOR LEADIN' ME ON —
WHEN SHE LOOKED AT ME
SHE WAS AS GOOD AS
GONE.

So I followed her and her pinstriped john. Palmetto Lounge. Upscale dive.

Where Baby performed. Oh yeah … Baby performed … *(Inside the Palmetto Lounge: The Wife performs with a band. The Husband sits at a table, martini in front of him. The Thief makes his way over and joins him.)*

THE WIFE.

> FRIDAY NIGHT DOWN ON HOUSTON
> IN A SPOT CALLED BAMBOO JACK'S
> EVERYONE WAS DOIN' THE MAMBO
> AND DRINKIN' GOLDEN CADILLACS.
> SALLY WAS THERE WITH HER DADDY.
> BUT DADDY WAS IN A FUNK
> 'CAUSE SALLY MET UP WITH AND TOOK A SHINE
> TO A HUNK FROM EAST PODUNK —
> DADDY CRIED, "HEY, WHATCHA DOIN', WHATCHA DOIN'!
> WHAT'S HE GOT I DON'T GOT?
> ALL I SEE'S
> AMERICAN CHEESE.
> HE'LL MELT WHEN YOU GET HOT."
> AND SALLY SAID:
> "I SEE WHAT I WANNA SEE.
> I KNOW WHAT I WANNA KNOW.
> I DON'T NEED YOU
> TO TELL ME WHAT'S TRUE
> IF YOU DON'T LIKE IT, DADDY
> YOU CAN BLOW, BLOW, BLOW, BLOW,
> BLOW!"

THE THIEF.

(To the husband.)

> EVER SEEN A BABY LIKE THAT?
> SHAKIN' HER ASS LIKE THAT.
> THEY DON'T MAKE TITS LIKE THAT.

Gives me the ole Bethlehem Steel. Who is she?

THE HUSBAND. My wife.

THE WIFE.

> SATURDAY NIGHT AT THE SAME PLACE.
> THEY ROLL UP THE BAMBOO RUG.
> EVERYONE WAS DOIN' THE LIMBO
> EXCEPT FOR SALLY AND HER PODUNK PLUG.

SEEMS HE TOOK A SHINE TO SOME CHICKEN
SHAKIN' HER TOM-TOM-TOM.
SALLY SAW THAT AND — GUACAMOLE —
SHE EXPLODED LIKE THE HYDROGEN BOMB.
SHE CRIED, "HEY, HEY, WHATCHA DOIN', WHATCHA DOIN'?
WHAT'S SHE GOT THAT I LACK?
THAT CHICKEN IS THIN
AND MEANER THAN SIN
AND UGLIER THAN BAMBOO JACK!"

THE HUSBAND and BAND.
AND HE SAID!

THE WIFE.
"I SEE WHAT I WANNA SEE
I KNOW WHAT I WANNA KNOW.
I DON'T NEED YOU
TO TELL ME WHAT'S TRUE
IF YOU DON'T LIKE IT, BABY,
YOU CAN BLOW BLOW BLOW BLOW
BLOW BLOW BLOW BLOW!
I SEE WHAT I WANNA SEE
I KNOW WHAT I WANNA KNOW
I DON'T NEED YOU
TO TELL ME WHAT'S TRUE —
IF YOU DON'T LIKE IT BABY BABY BABY BABY BABY
YOU CAN BLOW!"

(She finishes her number and exits. The Thief strikes up a conversation with the Husband.)

THE THIEF. Buy you a drink?

THE HUSBAND. Vodka martini, very dry, straight up, three olives.

THE THIEF. *(Out.)* To get her, I had to get him. Killing him wasn't part of the plan. Thought I could get rid of him in other ways. Two drinks later — *(To the Husband.)* Whatcha say you do?

THE HUSBAND. Taxis.

THE THIEF. I used to drive, too. But the customers got to me.

THE HUSBAND. I own taxis.

THE THIEF. Oh. A lot?

THE HUSBAND. A lot.

THE THIEF. You know the Vecchio brothers?

THE HUSBAND. No.

THE THIEF. I do work for them. Maybe you heard of me? Jimmy Mako?

THE HUSBAND. No.

THE THIEF. Yeah, and I know a few things.

THE HUSBAND. Yeah?

THE THIEF. Yeah. I know where they stashed things.

THE HUSBAND. Things?

THE THIEF. Cash they don't want some people to know about. But I know about it. I know exactly where it is.

THE HUSBAND. Cash?

THE THIEF. Cash cash. *(Spoken, in rhythm.)*

> There's a little boathouse …
> Right asides the pond …
> Over by the statue …
> Couple steps beyond.
> Cash.

THE HUSBAND. So?

THE THIEF. So, too bad it's just sittin' there. If someone were to dig it up, well, nobody'd know it was missing. Not for a while, at least.

THE HUSBAND. No thanks.

THE THIEF. Cryin' shame. All that cash could be ours. You wouldn't have to do anything. I need a lookout. An earwig.

THE HUSBAND. You think I'd let a stranger take me into Central Park in the middle of the night to steal someone's cash? What do you take me for?

THE THIEF. *(Calling to a waitress, off.)* Two more vodka martinis. Very, very dry. Straight up. Three olives. *(During the following, the Thief feeds the Husband countless martinis [figuratively].)*

> BIG MONEY.
> WAITIN' FOR THE TAKIN'
> BIG MONEY.
> IT'S YOUR LUCKY DAY.
> YOUR MONEY.
> UP TO US TO GRAB IT.
> YOU WANNA, WE CAN CAB IT,
> I'LL LEAD THE WAY.
> YOU KNOW YOU NEED MONEY
> TO KEEP YOUR BABY HAPPY.
> COLD MONEY.
> TO KEEP HER IN THE ICE.

WELL, THERE'S BIG MONEY.
JUST HOLD OUT YOUR MITTEN
BRING ALONG THE KITTEN
AND DON'T THINK TWICE.
YOU DON'T KNOW ME FROM ADAM
BUT WE BOTH WAS BORN OF EVE.
AND YOU CAN COUNT ON ME, BROTHER,
WHEN I SAY YOU MUST BELIEVE
THAT THERE IS —
THE HUSBAND.
(Loudly.)
BIG MONEY.
THE THIEF. Shhhh —
KEEP IT TO YOURSELF, MAN.
HARD MONEY
EASY TO BE GOT.
THE THIEF and THE HUSBAND.
OUR MONEY.
THE THIEF.
CHEW ON IT AND SWALLOW.
ALL YOU DO IS FOLLOW,
I'LL LEAD THE WAY.
I'LL LEAD THE WAY.
GONNA EAT THAT OLIVE?
Mind if I?
AIN'T AMERICA A FABULOUS PLACE?
THERE'S GOLD BAKED RIGHT INTO
MOM'S APPLE PIE.
AIN'T AMERICA A GODDAMN BLESSED PLACE?
THERE'S GRAVY POURIN' OUT OF THE RED, WHITE AND BLUE-
CHIP
SKY...!
THE HUSBAND.
BIG MONEY.
THE THIEF.
HIS GREEDY LITTLE MIND WENT.
THE HUSBAND.
BIG MONEY?

19

THE THIEF.
    PINGY-PANGY PONG.
THE THIEF and THE HUSBAND.
    OUR MONEY.
THE THIEF.
    LET'S SAY JUST SUPPOSIN'
    I MEET YOU AFTER CLOSIN'
    YOU CAN'T GO WRONG.

    AND IF YOU'RE WANTIN' MAYBE
    WHY NOT BRING ALONG THE BABY — THE WIFE —
    ALONG.
    I'LL LEAD THE WAY; I'LL LEAD THE WAY …
(The Husband rises to join the Thief. The scene shifts from the lounge to the park. Note: all action is suggested and stylized — not to be taken literally, in the tradition of Japanese Kabuki.)
THE THIEF. She didn't wanna come along, but in his condition, she didn't want to leave him alone. It was too perfect.
    CENTRAL PARK.
    JUNGLELAND.
    HIDDEN TREASURES
    FOR GREEDY FISHES.
    THE BABY DIDN'T LIKE IT.
    THE BABY DIDN'T TRUST ME.
    MADE ME MORE THAN HORNY …
I told her to wait in the clearing; her husband and me'd be right back.
    NO STARS.
    THE JUNGLE'S BLACK …
And I led him down into the bushes.
    DOWN INTO THE BOATHOUSE.
    RIGHT ASIDES THE POND.
    OVER BY THE STATUE
    COUPLA STEPS BEYOND …
Then I cracked him on the head. And with an electrical cord I keep with me for special occasions, I tied him up. Then I went back to the wifey. Told her there'd been an accident and she was needed — *(The Wife appears. She reacts to seeing the Husband bound by electrical wire.)*
THE WIFE. Louie!
THE THIEF.
    BABY'S GONNA DANCE TONIGHT!

THE WIFE. Louie!

THE THIEF.

    BABY'S GONNA GET IT FOR FREE —

THE WIFE. Sonofabitch — stay away —

THE THIEF.

    BABY'S GONNA ROCK AND ROLL AND DO THE DO —

(She roars in anger and pulls out a stiletto.) Well. What's that?

THE WIFE. Stay away from me. *(Smirking, he goes to her. She lunges at him. He overpowers her quickly, twisting her arm and bringing her to surrender.)*

THE THIEF.

(Out.)

    YOU WANNA KNOW HOW GOOD SHE WAS?

    YOU WANNA KNOW HOW GOOD I WAS?

Whadaya think? After. After …

    COLD.

    CHILLY.

    EYES LIKE A DEMON.

    HOT.

    BURNING.

You wanted this. Oh yes you did. Tell the truth.

THE WIFE. Louie …

THE THIEF.

    I SEE WHAT I WANNA SEE

    I KNOW WHAT I WANNA KNOW.

    I DON'T NEED YOU

    TO TELL ME WHAT'S TRUE

    IF YOU DON'T LIKE IT, BABY,

    YOU, YOU …

    YOU'LL GO AWAY WITH ME.

    YOU KNOW YOU WILL.

    YOU'LL GO AWAY WITH ME.

    AND NOT LOOK BACK.

    DOES THE SUN REALLY RISE IN THE EAST?

    DOES THE EARTH REALLY SPIN AROUND THE SUN?

    WHAT'S IT MATTER IN THE LEAST.

    WHAT'S REAL FOR ME AIN'T REAL FOR EVERYONE.

    YOU WANNA STAY WITH ME.

    YOU KNOW YOU DO.

YOU KNOW THE TRUTH
IS TEARIN' UP YOUR HEART.
YOU KNEW WHAT YOU NEEDED.
YOU KNEW WHAT YOU WANTED TO FIND.
YOU'LL GO AWAY WITH ME
AND LEAVE WHAT WAS BEHIND ...

THE WIFE. Kill me. Or kill my husband. Or let him fight you. Whichever one of you wins can have me. It doesn't matter. Go on. Coward. Coward. Coward.

THE THIEF. Baby wants a fight, huh? Baby likes that. I like that. I had a ten-inch blade on me. For extra-special occasions: A fair and square and fuckin' honorable fight to the death! *(The Thief goes to the husband and slices away the cord.)* Good morning, Mr. Pinstripe. Time to eat your breakfast.

(The Thief tosses his knife to the Husband. The Thief takes up the Wife's stiletto. The Husband rises and attacks. It's a colorful fight, but one the Husband loses. The Thief stabs him through the heart. The Husband collapses. The Wife howls and runs off into the park. The Thief stands over the body, licks the tip of his knife. The scene fades away. The Thief is in the police station again.)

THE THIEF. Jimmy Mako — thief extraordina-rio. 1951 will be remembered as the year Jimmy Mako terrorized New York. Won't it? Didn't see where the baby ran off to, probably to call you bluebears. The knife? Threw it in the pond. Her stiletto? By the statue. Why the hell you makin' me repeat myself? You don't believe me?

SO WHATCHA WANT ME TO SAY?
I TOLD YA.
I KILLED HIM.
BELIEVE WHATCHA WANNA BELIEVE.
WHAT DO I CARE?
YOU WANT THE TRUTH.
SO HERE: TAKE THE TRUTH.
I'LL TAKE THE CHAIR.

(The Thief disappears and is replaced with the Janitor. The Janitor is more upset, more fatigued by the interrogation.)

THE JANITOR. Okay okay okay, I did see him, okay? Okay I did see him ... I wasn't lying. I just — I can't think straight anymores, you guys are pooping me out — okay, I know! But ... some things you remember, some things you don't remember. I didn't see him kill him, I told you that. I saw the body, that's all. That's the whole point of this, right? The body? I told you, the guy was dead. And I did exactly what you're supposed to do in situations like this: I went home.

IN THIS TOWN
ONE THING LEADS TO ANOTHER
THEN ANOTHER
AND THEN ANOTHER
ONE THING LEADS TO ANOTHER.
BEST NOT TO GET INVOLVED.
IN THIS TOWN
SOME GUY'S ALWAYS GOT A BROTHER
WHO'S A BROTHER
WHO'S GOT A BROTHER
WHO'D EASILY SHOOT HIS OWN MOTHER
BEST NOT TO GET INVOLVED.
YOU NEVER KNOW
WHEN YOU BUMP INTO A STIFF
WHOSE STIFF IT IS
AND HOW IT GOT THERE.
MYSTERIES ALL GOT AN UNDERTOW.
AND WHEN YOU GO
SNOOPIN' ROUND THE FACTS
THE FACTS MAY TURN OUT
TO BE STRANGER
THAN THE MYSTERY YOU WASN'T S'POSE TO KNOW —
DON'T STOP.
DON'T TOUCH.
DON'T ASK.
GO HOME GO HOME GO HOME —

IN THIS TOWN
ONE THING LEADS TO ANOTHER
THEN ANOTHER
AND THEN ANOTHER.
LIVIN' HERE YOU GOTTA SMOTHER
YOUR CURIOSITY —
WAIT UNTIL THE MYSTERY'S SOLVED.
BEST NOT TO GET, BEST NOT TO GET,
BEST NOT TO GET INVOLVED.

(The Wife appears, replacing the Janitor.)

THE WIFE.
 WHAT DO YOU WANT ME TO SAY?
 I KILLED HIM.
 MY HUSBAND.
 LOOK AT ME.
 WHAT CAN I DO?
 LOOK AT ME …
It's in the papers. I told my story over and over again to you people — *(She cries.)* I'm sorry. *(A beat. She composes herself.)* We'd been to a movie earlier that night. I loved our movie nights — it's one of the things I love most about Louie — *(She cries.)* I'm sorry. I won't cry again. It's just … he took such good care of me, my Louie did: picking out my clothes, helping my career, making me … better. He loved and honored me, don't you understand that? I tried my best to honor him. I tried … but … After that monster — after he … I must have blacked out. When I woke up it was near morning. I could hear little animals crackling in the leaves … And I saw Louie. He was alive. Where was the monster who…? I don't know. I saw Louie. He was alive, but … *(The park reappears — perhaps from a slightly different angle. The Husband is tied up, facing the Wife. He is silent, glaring at her coldly.)*
 HE LOOKED AT ME
 SILENT AS A STATUE.
 HE LOOKED AT ME.
 A LOOK I'D NEVER SEEN BEFORE.
 COLD AND HOT —
 GLARING IN THE DARK.
 FREEZING MY INSIDES —
 BURNING DOWN THE PARK —
 I FELT UNCLEAN. I FELT —
Unclean. He'd watched everything. And all that we'd ever been was gone. Gone. *(She crawls closer to her Husband.)* Say something … Louie? Say something. Don't look at me that way. *(She spies the stiletto. She cuts her Husband's bonds. She places the knife in his hand.)* Kill me … Kill me! That's what you want! Do it! Do it!!! *(He does nothing.)* My love. My love my love my love …
 REMEMBER WHERE YOU FOUND ME?
 WORKING AS A HATCHECK.
 SLUMMING WITH A GAMBLER.
 LOST.
 REMEMBER HOW YOU SAVED ME?
 YOU BOUGHT ME YELLOW ROSES.
 I REMEMBER CRYING;

HOW MUCH DID THEY COST?
LOUIE, MY SAVIOR.
LOUIE, MY HERO.
WHERE ARE YOU NOW?
LOUIE, MY ANGEL.
LOUIE, MY HUSBAND.
DIDN'T I VOW
TO LOVE AND OBEY?
TELL ME WHAT TO DO.
I'LL DO AS YOU SAY …

THE HUSBAND. Together.

THE WIFE. Together — ?

THE HUSBAND. Together. *(He offers her the knife. They're to die together. A beat.)*

THE WIFE.
I WOULD DIE WITH YOU.
HOW EASILY I WOULD.
TOGETHER WE FOUND
IN THIS SORROWFUL CITY
A GARDEN OF GOOD.
TOGETHER. TOGETHER. TOGETHER —
NOTHING TO BE SCARED OF,
NOT IF WE'RE TOGETHER.
REMEMBER WHAT YOU TOLD ME?
WE GO ON FOREVER.
HUNDRED BILLION LIFETIMES.
THIS IS ONLY ONE.
LOUIE, MY SAVIOR.
LOUIE, MY HERO.
LOOK AT US NOW.
LOUIE, I'M READY.
LOUIE, MY HUSBAND.
WE ARE NO MORE.
BOTH OF US THROUGH.
LOUIE, GUIDE MY HAND.
I WILL HONOR YOU.
I WILL HONOR YOU
I WILL HONOR YOU
I WILL HONOR YOU
I WILL HONOR YOU —

(She plunges the knife into his chest. They arch, as in an orgasm. She pulls away. She lets the knife drop to the ground. The scene disappears. She is back in the police station.) But you see … I was too afraid to kill myself. … Later, I tried. First with pills … Then I tried to throw myself into the river. But … I don't know … there's too much life left in me … I don't know …

    WHAT DO YOU WANT ME TO SAY?

    LOOK AT ME.

I was raped! My husband is dead!

    LOOK AT ME.

    LOOK AT ME …

(She disappears. The Janitor reappears.)

THE JANITOR. Her … She was beautiful, yeah. So I didn't mention her — I know, I know — She … I know. How can you forget something like her? She was … Some women are your normal women. But some women. They can look at blood and get hungry. This woman, she was hungry, oh yeah. I know, I know, I'm not a psychic so how do I know what she was thinking when she — when he … They say only the dead tell the truth, you know. *(He disappears into the shadows as the Medium appears.)*

THE MEDIUM.

    WHAT WOULD YOU LIKE ME TO SAY?

    IT'S MY WORK.

    TALKING WITH THE DEAD.

    FLAT RATE.

    TWENTY BUCKS.

    SO THERE I WAS: I'M HOLDING A SÉANCE.

    FOR A LAWYER.

    WHO IS DESP'RATE.

    WANTS TO SPEAK WITH A LOVED ONE:

    HIS SISTER ALICE SUE.

    ALICE MAE.

I was trying to contact said deceased relative when this other spirit breaks in and I almost whooped my pants. I've heard about this happening to other mediums — psychic interruptions — but never to me.

    SO THIS SPIRIT — HE'S GOT A STORY

    IT'S A DOOZY —

    AND HE TELLS ME

    NO ONE ELSE KNOWS HIS STORY.

    THOUGHT I SHOULD GET INVOLVED.

Which is why I am here and providing my services for free. Which is what any honorable member of my profession would do. He came from the other side. This man. The husband. And so … restless … *(The Husband appears.)*

THE MEDIUM and THE HUSBAND.

> DARK …
>
> IT'S DARK HERE …
>
> SPACE …
>
> NO STARS …
>
> NOWHERE …
>
> I REMEMBER …
>
> MY LIFE …
>
> MY DEATH …

THE HUSBAND. My mother was wrong when she warned me that I would regret marrying a cheap lounge act for the rest of my life. I'll be regretting it for the rest of my death. Lily. My Lily. Okay. I was stupid. I shouldn't have trusted the guy. As a successful businessman I thought I was a good judge of character. Then again, I was plastered.

> BIG MONEY.
>
> HIDDEN IN A BOATHOUSE.
>
> HOT MONEY
>
> SOMEWHERE IN THE DARK.
>
> MY MONEY.
>
> HAD TO TRUST A STRANGER
>
> HELL, I KNEW THE DANGER
>
> WHEN WE HIT THE PARK …

When he *took* her. She *went* with him. She was afraid, my wife, my Lily, but she … *went* with him. Like … As though she had always wanted to — and all that love, honor and obey crap went right down the toilet. I felt myself leave my body. I tried to think about something else — train my mind on something other than their — lovemaking. I thought about the movie I'd seen that night. *Rashomon*. *Rashomon*. Such a beautiful film. She fell asleep during it. My wife doesn't like foreign movies. But me — I need the cinema. When all you do all day is talk taxis and drivers, hey, you need some sort of release. I put my mind elsewhere. The marquee outside the theatre was missing an "A" from the title, so it spelled "R shomon." Where had the "A" on the marquee gone? Gone … *(As the Husband continues, the Wife and the Thief appear, rapt in mutual seduction. They make love passionately, in front of the Husband.)*

THE HUSBAND. "A" for Anger. Ambition.

> ANDREW SISTERS.
>
> AMERICA …

THE WIFE and THE THIEF.
    I'LL (YOU'LL) GO AWAY WITH YOU (ME)
    I DON'T CARE WHERE (YOU KNOW YOU WILL)
THE HUSBAND and THE MEDIUM.
    ALARM.
THE WIFE and THE THIEF.
    I'LL (YOU'LL) GO AWAY WITH YOU (ME)
    AND NOT LOOK BACK.
THE HUSBAND and THE MEDIUM.
    AMNESIA.
THE WIFE and THE THIEF.
    DOES THE SUN REALLY RISE IN THE EAST?
    DOES THE EARTH REALLY SPIN AROUND THE SUN?
    WHAT'S IT MATTER IN THE LEAST? (IT DON'T MATTER)
    WHAT'S REAL FOR ME AIN'T REAL FOR EVERYONE.
THE HUSBAND and THE MEDIUM.
    ACTRESS. ASSHOLE.
THE WIFE and THE THIEF.
    I (YOU) WANT TO STAY WITH YOU (ME)
    I DON'T HAVE A CHOICE. (YOU KNOW YOU DO,
    YOU KNOW YOU DO.)
THE HUSBAND and THE MEDIUM.
    ABANDONED. ANNULMENT.
THE WIFE.
    YOU TOOK AWAY MY RIGHT
    TO THINK AND CHOOSE —
THE THIEF.
    YOU KNOW THE TRUTH.
THE HUSBAND and THE MEDIUM.
    ADULTERY. AMBIVALENCE. ACHE. ABASE.
THE WIFE and THE THIEF.
    YOU KNEW WHAT I NEEDED
    YOU KNEW WHAT I WANTED TO FIND
THE HUSBAND and THE MEDIUM.
    ART. ARTIFICE. ALL GONE.
THE WIFE and THE THIEF.
    I'LL (YOU'LL) GO AWAY WITH YOU (ME)
THE HUSBAND and THE MEDIUM.
    GONE.

THE WIFE and THE THIEF.
   AND LEAVE WHAT WAS
   BEHIND.
THE HUSBAND.
   GONE … GONE …
THE WIFE. Do something for me.
THE THIEF. Anything.
THE WIFE. This man thinks I'm his property.
THE MEDIUM.
   LOOK AT HER EYES —
THE HUSBAND.
   LOOK AT HER EYES
THE THIEF.
   LOOK AT YOUR EYES …
THE WIFE. *(To her husband.)* But I am not your property.
THE THIEF.
   ICY HEAT.
THE HUSBAND.
   ICY HEAT.
THE MEDIUM.
   ICY HEAT.
THE WIFE. *(To her husband.)* I'll never have any peace as long as you're around.
(She giggles, evil.)
THE HUSBAND.
   A DEVIL RELEASED.
THE THIEF.
   A DEVIL RELEASED.
THE HUSBAND, THIEF and MEDIUM.
   A DEVIL RELEASED …
THE WIFE.
   NO MORE TRYING NOT TO LAUGH
   AS YOU STRUGGLE
   TO SQUEEZE INTO YOUR TROUSERS
   AS YOU SLOWLY GO BALD.
   NO MORE LISTENING TO DANNY KAYE ALBUMS
   OR LEAPING TO YOUR VOICE
   OR JUMPING WHEN CALLED.
   NO MORE SLEEPING THROUGH
   YOUR BORING FOREIGN MOVIES —

WHAT WAS IT? THE LAST TIME?
SOMETHING JAPANESE.
NO MORE SITTING STILL
WHILE YOU AND ALL YOUR LAWYERS
DRONE ON AND ON
ABOUT TAXICAB FEES.
NO MORE VISITING YOUR MOTHER EVERY SUNDAY
CHOKING DOWN HER PASTA
WHICH SHE ALWAYS OVERSALTS.
NO MORE 3 A.M. JEALOUS INNUENDOS
THEN BEGGING MY FORGIVENESS
AND THEN POINTING OUT MY FAULTS.

NO MORE
NO MORE
DON'T LOOK AT ME THAT WAY.
YOUR EARS AND YOUR EYES
GOT USED TO THE LIES
BUT YOU'RE GETTING THE TRUTH TODAY.

NO MORE FORCING ME
TO WEAR THE CRAP YOU BUY ME.
HAS ANYBODY TOLD YOU
YOU HAVE ROTTEN TASTE IN CLOTHES?
NO MORE FORCING ME TO DO
AND NOT TO QUESTION.
WHY I TOOK IT THIS LONG,
CHRIST ONLY KNOWS.
NO MORE FORCING ME
TO GIVE UP WHAT I WANTED.
SURE, I LIKED YOUR MONEY
BUT YOU NEVER BOUGHT MY SOUL.
NO MORE FORCING ME
TO PUT UP WITH YOUR PATRONIZING
HOT-STICK, KING-KONG
NEED TO CONTROL
NO MORE FORCING ME
TO ACT LIKE I ENJOY IT
WHEN YOU SUDDENLY REMEMBER

THAT YOU'RE SHARING MY BED.
NO MORE FORCING ME
TO LIE AND SAY I'M SORRY.
YOU WANNA BLAME ME, BABY
WELL THEN, YOU GO RIGHT AHEAD.

NO MORE.
NO MORE.
DON'T LOOK AT ME THAT WAY.
YOU'RE NOT ALIVE.
WE'RE NOT ALIVE.
YOU AND I DIED TODAY.
NO, NO MORE.
NO MORE.
NO MORE!
NO MORE!

Kill him! *(The Thief goes over to the Husband and unties him. The Husband doesn't move. The Thief goes back to the Wife and hugs her tight.)*

THE THIEF. So, man. What is it? *(Suddenly holding the stiletto to her throat.)* You want me to slash her throat now and save you the trouble later?

THE WIFE. Wha — kill him!

THE THIEF. Shut up. *(To the Husband.)* You want me to gut this bitch? Nod your head or wiggle your toes or something. I'll be glad to do it.

THE WIFE. *(Hysterical.)* No! Louie!

THE THIEF. She ain't worth it. So be it. I'll let you do it yourself. Jesus. She's got more killer in her than me. *(The Thief throws the stiletto into the Husband's lap and exits.)*

THE WIFE. Louie? Don't look at me that way … Don't look at — *(She whimpers and crawls away backwards like a harmed animal. She cries and runs off.)*

THE HUSBAND.
   SOMEONE WAS CRYING
   SOMEONE IN THE DARK.

Me … Her stiletto … I bought it for her. For protection.
   LILY, MY TREASURE
   LILY, MY JUDAS …

(He picks up the stiletto.)
   SIMPLE TO DO
   LEAVING THE WORLD.
   SIMPLE AS THIS.

THE HUSBAND and THE MEDIUM.
SIMPLE AS THIS
EASIER DONE
THAN TO CONCIEVE;
DON'T HAVE TO THINK.
NOTHING TO GRIEVE.

LIFE TRIES TOO HARD
TO IMITATE ART.
DEATH DOESN'T HAVE TO.
IT CUTS TO THE HEART
AND ANSWERS WITH TRUTH:
TO LIVE, YOU MUST LIE.
HONOR DEMANDS
THE HERO MUST DIE.
SIMPLE AS THIS.
SIMPLE AS THIS.
SIMPLE AS …

(He puts the stiletto to his chest and swiftly plunges it in.)

THE HUSBAND. I should have bought her a gun instead. Would've been quicker. Dying took a long time. Later, I felt someone —

THE MEDIUM. I felt someone —

THE HUSBAND. Pull the stiletto out of me —

THE MEDIUM. Pull the stiletto out —

THE HUSBAND. Someone slipped it out —

THE MEDIUM. Someone —

THE HUSBAND. And all my blood flowed into the grass …

THE HUSBAND and THE MEDIUM.
DARK …
IT'S DARK HERE …
SPACE …
NO STARS …
NOWHERE …

THE MEDIUM.
AND THAT WAS ALL I RECEIVED.
I'M JUST REPEATING HIS WORDS.
I'M JUST A FILTER, OKAY?
I ONLY TOLD YOU THE TRUTH.

(The Janitor reappears. The Husband and the Medium fade away.)

THE JANITOR. It's morning outside, isn't it? I can feel it. I can feel the sun ris-

ing. The truth is: A man's dead and I didn't do nothing to stop it. The truth is …
I'll never be able to take my shortcut home through the park anymores — after what
I saw, it's ruined for me. This city can be so beautiful and so mean … Okay … I'll
start over … Big premiere … 5 A.M. … Sunday morning … *(The Janitor is now in
the park. During the following, he reenacts coming upon the body of the Husband, still
alive. The Janitor pulls the knife from the Husband's body and the Husband dies.)*

LIGHT IN THE EAST
GOT A NEW DAY
IF YOU LISTEN YOU CAN HEAR IT
MILES AND MILES AWAY:
THE LOW, LOW RUMBLE
OF THE TOWN WAKIN' UP
WITH THE LIGHT IN THE EAST
NIGHT IN THE WEST.
THERE'S THE MOON ALL PALE AND TIRED
LIKE SHE NEEDS A LITTLE REST
'CAUSE THE NIGHT'S BEEN BUSY
YOU CAN HEAR IT ECHO:
BOUNCIN' OFFA BUILDINGS LIKE A GHOST
YEAH, THE NIGHT'S BEEN BUSY
TEARIN' UP THE CITY
LIKE A TOO-DRUNK GUEST
WHO STEALS FROM HIS HOST
AND LEAVES BEHIND
BLEARY EYES.
THE SMELL OF SEX
AND WHISKEY LIES …
THEN COMES THE LIGHT IN THE EAST
TIME I LIKE BEST.
IT'S BETTER WHEN THE DAY
STILL HAS ITS YOUTH.
BETTER TO WALK.
BETTER TO BREATHE.
BETTER TO SEE

THE JANITOR.	THE MEDIUM.
THE TRUTH	AND THAT WAS ALL THAT HE SAID
THE PARK.	I'M JUST REPEATING HIS WORDS.
A STATUE.	YOU EVER TALK TO THE DEAD?
A THIEF.	I ONLY TOLD YOU THE TRUTH.

JANITOR/MEDIUM.

THE TRUTH.
    THE TRUTH
HIS WIFE.
    HIS WORDS.
HER BEAUTY.
    HIS SPIRIT.
A SCARF.
    THE DARK.

JANITOR/MEDIUM/THIEF.

THE TRUTH
    THE TRUTH
        THE TRUTH
HER KNIFE.
    A THIEF.
        HER EYES.
A BOATHOUSE.
    A WOMAN.
        HER BODY.
HIS BLOOD.
    HIS BLOOD.
        HER KNIFE.

JANITOR/MEDIUM/THIEF/WIFE.

THE TRUTH
    THE TRUTH
        THE TRUTH
            THE TRUTH
A LIE.
    HER KNIFE.
        HER SKIN.
            MY LOVE.
HER HUSBAND.
    A STATUE.
        HER TEMPER.
            MY HUSBAND.

THE DARK.
    A LIE.
        A FOOL.
            THE TRUTH.

THE THIEF.

IT HAPPENED JUST AS I SAID.

WHAT GOOD IS LYING TO YOU?

I'LL GET THE CHAIR ANYWAY.

I ONLY TOLD YOU THE TRUTH.

THE WIFE.

WHAT DO YOU WANT ME TO SAY?

I TRIED THE BEST I KNOW HOW.

I TOLD YOU ALL THAT I KNOW.

I ONLY TOLD YOU THE TRUTH.

THE HUSBAND.

THERE'S NOTHING MORE AFTER THAT.

THERE'S NOTHING MORE THAT I KNEW.

THERE'S NOTHING MORE OF MY LIFE.

I ONLY TOLD YOU THE TRUTH.

THE JANITOR/MEDIUM/HUSBAND/THIEF/WIFE.
    THE TRUTH
    THE TRUTH
    THE TRUTH
    THE TRUTH
    THE TRUTH.

    THE TRUTH
    THE TRUTH
    THE TRUTH
    THE TRUTH
    THE TRUTH.
ALL.
    THE TRUTH — THE TRUTH — THE TRUTH — THE TRUTH —
    THE … TRUTH …
(Lights.)

End of Act One

ACT TWO

KESA AND MORITO (MORITO)

Morito appears. He is a handsome predator. Kesa appears. Kesa is a beauti-
ful, sensual monster. Morito prepares to meet his lover. We hear his thoughts;
his lover does not.

MORITO.
    TONIGHT I KISS MY LOVER
    FOR THE LAST TIME.
    I GO TO HER AT MIDNIGHT;
    SLIPPING PAST THE GATE
    FLOATING TO HER BED
    I LET HER HANDS CARESS ME
    FOR THE LAST TIME

    I KNIFE INTO HER BODY
    FORCIBLY AND PROUD;
    (SHE SAYS THAT I'M INCREDIBLY ENDOWED.
    THICKER THAN HER HUSBAND.)

    AND AS I KISS MY LOVER
    FOR THE LAST TIME
    THE WORLD DISSOLVES
    AROUND ME
    I DESERT MY BODY
    ALL OF TIME IS GONE.

    DUSK IS DAWN;
    DAWN IS NOON;
    LATE IS NOW;
    NOW IS SOON
    THIS IS WHAT IT'S LIKE TO BE GOD.

I WATCH MYSELF OUTSIDE MYSELF:
SLEEP AND BREATHE AND WAKE AND CRY,
SWEAT AND SHIT AND SCREW AND LIE —
MY GOD, IT'S HELL TO BE GOD.

WATCHING FROM A DISTANCE
I NEITHER LAUGH NOR CRY
AS THE FLOODGATES ARE OPENED
AND THE INNOCENT DIE
A LIE BECOMES THE TRUTH
AND THE TRUTH BECOMES A LIE.
LIE …
LIE.

TONIGHT I KISS MY LOVER
FOR THE LAST TIME.
SHE'LL FEEL MY HANDS ABOUT HER,
TIGHT AROUND HER THROAT;
I'LL END MY LOVER'S LIFE.

AND I'LL RETURN TO MY BODY;
TO MY BONES, TO MY SKIN;
WHAT I'VE SET IN MOTION
CANNOT BE REVERSED.
TIME WILL BEGIN
TIME
TIME
TIME!

(Embracing his lover, Morito smiles as he grips Kesa tightly around her throat and kisses her. At the music's climax, he begins to strangle his lover. Kesa reveals a gleaming knife, preparing to stab him. Immediate blackout.)

GLORYDAY

The Priest appears. He is in conference with his superior. Note: As with R
Shomon, *the simplest of sets should be employed: two chairs; perhaps a row
of reed plants, to suggest the park.*

PRIEST. Yes. I've put on the collar again. But no … I'm not celebrating Mass.
Not … yet, Monsignor. Maybe, in time…? My life, now, is … is like … a sen-
tence in which every word seems to be missing a letter.
CONFESSORS. *(Heard, off.)*
  BLESS ME FATHER, I HAVE SINNED
  MY LAST CONFESSION WAS …
PRIEST. You've been very gracious to me, Monsignor, very patient. I haven't been
able to speak about what happened. It's time to. Time. *(Appearing in shadow,
Confessors question the priest.)*
CONFESSORS.
  BLESS ME FATHER … (Why? It makes no sense.)
  BLESS ME FATHER … (Is it some sort of punishment for my sins?)
  BLESS ME FATHER … (Why doesn't God help me?)
  BLESS ME FATHER …
PRIEST. I was eighteen when I entered the seminary. I kept my vows. I was celi-
bate — and how many priests can say that? And I loved God. I loved those who
love God. But … What had constituted my calling disappeared, gradually — it
wasn't kicked out of me — even though the tragedy that hit this city could have
contributed, but I'm not going to blame that for — but, Monsignor, I couldn't
cope with all the … need? I was helpless and I couldn't feel my faith. It just …
Evaporated. Poof.
  LAST YEAR.
  LAST YEAR.
  I SAW THE WORLD EXPLODING.
  I FELT A WEIRD FOREBODING
  BEFORE I WATCHED THE CITY FALL
  IN SILVER CLOUDS
  CONSUMING CROWDS
  OF UNSUSPECTING SOULS.

(The Confessors confront the Priest.)

A YOUNG WOMAN. I begged them to keep looking for his body — even months after — I still don't believe that he's dead.

PRIEST. God understands your grief. You can't give up on hope …

A YOUNG MAN. I left Mark and Grace and that Korean woman, Kim-something? — I just left them in the stairwell and ran — and now they're dead and I'm — Father, I don't think God will ever forgive me.

PRIEST. God will forgive you. You have to have faith.

AN OLDER MAN. I keep asking, "Why not?" Why not do myself in? I can't get the images out of my head: the bodies and, oh! The children — and the blood and that awful fire —

PRIEST. God is —

AN OLDER WOMAN. I don't understand why he had to die, Father. It makes no sense.

PRIEST. Of course it doesn't — not at this moment —

AN OLDER WOMAN. Then tell me why it happened?! Why?

PRIEST.

> HOW WRONG,
> I THOUGHT,
> THAT GOD WOULD HAVE NO PITY;
> HE'D LET A GLEAMING CITY
> BE CRUSHED AND LEVELLED TO THE GROUND.
> AROUND ME I HEARD PRAYING:
> CRIES OF GRIEF,
> AND PRAYING;
> BUT I REMEMBER SAYING: WHAT FOR?
> WHO IS LISTENING TO US?
> WHO HEARS OUR PRAYER?
> IS THERE SUCH A THING AS HEAVEN?
> IS THERE NO "THERE" THERE?
> LAST YEAR,
> LAST YEAR,
> BEFORE THE ENDLESS GRIEVING
> I WENT TO BED BELIEVING
> THAT GOD WOULD ALWAYS BE A FRIEND;
> BUT WHEN THE SMOKE FIN'LLY CLEARED,
> MY FAITH IN GOD HAD DISAPPEARED.

SO I LET GO OF HOPE.
AND THAT'S HOW I COULD COPE,
LAST YEAR.
LAST YEAR …

CONFESSORS.
BLESS ME FATHER
I HAVE SINNED
MY LAST CONFESSION WAS …

PRIEST. No — please, no more … I can't — I can't give anymore. There's nothing left to give …

CONFESSORS.
BLESS ME FATHER
TELL ME WHY (Is this some sort of punishment for my sins?)
ONLY THE BRAVE (The children — and the blood and the fire …)
AND INNOCENT DIE … (She was only nine years old …)

(The Priest pushes away from the smothering crowd. The Confessors disperse.)

PRIEST. Stop! I can't answer you! There isn't any answer! There was never an answer.

ALL THESE YEARS
I'VE BEEN LIVING A LIE,
A LIE, A LIE, A LIE, A LIE …

My Aunt Monica was right. *(The Priest's elderly Aunt Monica appears. She is a spitfire Italian woman.)*

AUNT.
RELIGION IS TYRANNY!

PRIEST. Born in Rome, she became a communist after Mussolini was deposed. Then she immigrated to America.

AUNT.
SALUTE THE WORKER!

PRIEST. A terrific cook —

AUNT.
SOCIALISM OR DIE!

PRIEST. And a dedicated atheist.

AUNT. You did *what?*

PRIEST. I remember how unhappy she was when I announced I was entering the priesthood. *(The Priest is now in his Aunt's kitchen. She feeds him.)*

AUNT. What did I tell you? You don't remember what I tell you.
THE GREATEST PRACTICAL JOKE
PLAYED ON THE COMMON FOLK

IS GOD.
You want some manicott'?
        THE WORST POLITICAL PRANK
        PULLED BY THE FILE AND RANK
        IS CHRIST-MOHAMMED-BUDDHA-VISHNU
        JOSEPH SMITH AND ALL HIS ANGELS —
        TO KEEP THE POOR IN CHECK
        THE BUSINESS OFFERS DAILY MASSES
        AND THREATENS HELL AND HECK.

        LOOK AT THE WORLD.
        YOU THINK THERE'S A GOD?
        THERE ISN'T A GOD.
        NOT WHEN YOU GOT ALL
        THOSE CRIMINAL TYPES
        LIKE HENRY KISSINGER
        SNEAKING AROUND
        AND PEDDLING NUKES.
        LOOK AT THE WORLD.
        IF THERE'S A GOD,
        YOU'D THINK HE'D DO SOMETHING TO STOP
        ALL THE WAR AND THE CRIME
        AND THE GRAFT
        AND HE'D PUNISH THOSE SONOVABITCHES
        WHO WRITE ALL THOSE
        STUPID NEW TV SHOWS.
        LOOK AT THE WORLD.
        THERE CAN'T BE A GOD.
        NOT WHEN YOU GOT
        THOSE CRAZY NUNS
        LIKE MOTHER THERESA
        WHO DON'T GIVE THOSE INDIANS RUBBERS
        AND SO THEY HAVE
        BABIES AND BABIES
        AND EV'RYONE'S CROWDED
        AND HUNGRY AND STARVING
        OF COURSE,
        IF INDIAN FOOD WAS ALL I HAD TO EAT.
        I WOULDN'T EAT.

PRIEST. Aunt Moni — this is a calling I've had. I can't turn my back when God speaks to me.

AUNT. God speaks to you. What's he sound like? Walter Cronkite? Ha.

PRIEST. You don't understand. It's a miracle: Don't you believe in the possibility that —

AUNT. No, I don't. Do you know how many millions of people have suffered and died because some crazy man said that God spoke to him?

PRIEST. I am not crazy.

AUNT.

>THERE'S LOTSA BLOOD YOU CAN SPILL;
>YOU'VE GOT THE RIGHT TO KILL
>FOR GOD.

Eat up, there's more lasagna —

>YOU'LL EARN YOUR SAINTLY REWARD
>AIMING YOUR MISSILES TOWARD
>THE HEATHEN WHO DO NOT BELIEVE IN
>ALL THE CRAP THAT YOU BELIEVE IN
>YOU WERE ALWAYS A GULLIBLE DOPE.
>YOU KEEP PLAYING DUMB
>AND BABY YOU'LL BE THE POPE.
>SO *MANGE!* FEAST, BEFORE YOU FALL
>FOR THE GREATEST PRACTICAL JOKE
>OF ALL!

(She kisses him, and sighs.) Madonn' ... *(She vanishes. The Priest is now in the park. It's near morning.)*

PRIEST. Aunt Monica was right all along. But I believed that I'd been called to Christ. Gullible dope. And the world is full of gullible dopes.

>LIGHT IN THE EAST.
>GOT A NEW DAY.
>IF YOU LISTEN YOU CAN HEAR IT
>MILES AND MILES AWAY ...

Central Park. So big. So ... central. People expect too much from their faith. They cry for absolution. As if they'd know what to do with it, if they had it. They want from *me,* absolution. Miracles. Christ.

>WHAT IF ...

Christ. All right ... Then I'll give you Christ ... *(He composes a message.)*

>*"IN THREE WEEKS*
>*ON TUESDAY*
>*AT ONE P.M. SHARP*

42

A MIRACLE WILL OCCUR.
HERE IN CENTRAL PARK
BEFORE OUR VERY EYES
FROM THE DEPTHS OF THE POND
CHRIST WILL RISE!
BELIEVE!
AND BE FREE!
BELIEVE AND BE FREE!"

There you go, folks. There's your miracle. Enjoy. *(He posts the announcement on the side of a tree. He settles himself on a bench not too far way. He observes people stopping to read it. Voices are heard, off.)*

VOICES.

"IN THREE WEEKS		
ON TUESDAY	*"IN THREE WEEKS*	
AT ONE P.M. SHARP	*ON TUESDAY*	*"IN THREE WEEKS*
A MIRACLE WILL OCCUR	*AT ONE P.M. SHARP*	*ON TUESDAY*
A MIRACLE!	*A MIRACLE WILL OCCUR*	*AT ONE P.M. SHARP*
A MIRACLE!"	*A MIRACLE!"*	*A MIRACLE!"*

PRIEST.
 ONE BY ONE
 THEY GATHER;
 STRANGERS IN THE PARK
 ONE BY ONE BY ONE
 THEY FLOCK LIKE CURIOUS CROWS
 AND THE LIE
 GROWS …

(The CPA appears. Or at least, a former CPA. He's "gone native," so to speak; It's as though he's taken his business suit and turned it into a bizarre tribal dashiki.)

CPA. Father! Have you read the message?

PRIEST. *(Aside.)* The more fragile makeup a person has, the more likely he or she will fall for the hoax — like a miniature A-bomb waiting to be detonated. Duck and cover … *(To the CPA.)* Yes! The message.

CPA. The Gloryday.

PRIEST. The Gloryday! Oh, that's good. We must spread the news. Tell all your friends! Tell all your family!

CPA. *(A beat.)* Father … on the Gloryday do you think that God will … notice me?

PRIEST. Oh, I think he'll notice you first thing.

CPA. You think I'm crazy, don't you?

PRIEST. Of course not.

CPA. Father ... do you think — and don't you lie to me: Will God see me again?

PRIEST. On the Gloryday ... all that has been lost ... will be found.

CPA. All that has been lost will be found.

    I WAS A CPA.
    OFFICE.
    BRIEFCASE.
    WHITE SHIRT.
    STRIPED TIE.
    CRUNCHING NUMBERS.
    HIDING ASSETS.
    TRYING TO DISGUISE
    MY CLIENTS' LITTLE LIES.

    I WAS A HAPPY MAN.
    NICE HOUSE.
    NICE LIFE.
    NICE KIDS.
    NICE WIFE.
    AND A GIRLFRIEND.
    I WAS KING OF MY DOMAIN.
    FORMULATING CAPITAL GAIN:
    TEN THOUSAND
    MINUS
    THREE THOUSAND
    DIVIDE BY
    SIX HUNDRED
    AND THAT'S ANOTHER MILLION!

    MY FATHER WAS A RABBI.
    AND I KNEW ABOUT GOD.
    I KNEW THAT GOD WATCHED ME
    DAY AND NIGHT.
    BUT THEN THE OTHER DAY,
    I WAS WORKING IN MY OFFICE,
    I WAS CRUNCHING LITTLE NUMBERS
    I WAS HIDING LITTLE LIES
    AND SUDDENLY I REALIZE THAT
    GOD DOESN'T SEE ME.

HE DOESN'T SEE ME THROUGH THE CONCRETE
OR THE BAD FLUORESCENT LIGHTING,
NO, GOD DOESN'T SEE ME.
HE DOESN'T SEE ME IN THE NUMBERS,
IN MY SUITS
OR IN MY LIFE!
HE DOESN'T SEE MY LIFE!

I tried to tell people but no one listened. Do you know what that's like when no one listens?

YOU GET ANGRY.
AT YOUR ASSHOLE BOSS.
AND YOUR STUPID WIFE
'CAUSE SHE CAN'T PERCEIVE
THE HELL YOU'RE GOING THROUGH,
AND THEN ONE DAY,
YOU WANNA BLOW HER FACE AWAY.
YOU WANNA BLOW THE WORLD AWAY!

SO I JUMPED IN A CAB
AND I DROVE THROUGH MANHATTAN
AND I REACHED COLUMBUS CIRCLE
AND I STOPPED.
AND I WALKED INTO THE PARK …

CENTRAL PARK.
JUNGLELAND.
HIDDEN TREASURES
FOR CPA'S.
AND CHEATING HUSBANDS
AND SONS OF RABBIS …

And I saw the message.
PRIEST. The Gloryday.
CPA. And I knew what I had to do.

HERE I AM IN CENTRAL PARK.
NO MORE JOB OR FAMILY.
NO MORE LIES.
OR SUITS OR TIES.
MADE MYSELF AT HOME HERE.
MADE MYSELF AT HOME.

AND ALL WEEK LONG
I HAVE SWAPPED CIGARETTES
FOR A SPOT ON A BENCH,
SLEEPING NEXT TO AN ACTOR
WHO SNORES.
(I LOVE IT.)

ALL WEEK LONG
I HAVE TANNED IN THE RAMBLES
AND BATHED IN THE POND;
I AM PERFUMED
WITH THE GREAT OUTDOORS!

WHO INVENTED CENTRAL PARK?
I WOULD LIKE TO THANK HIM.
GOD WILL SEE
A PURER ME:
GLORYDAY UNBIND ME;
PUT MY PAST BEHIND ME.
SHINE AND BLAZE AND BLIND ME!
COME AND FIND ME,
GOD!

(He exits.)

PRIEST. Like the dropping of a half-lit match on a dry forest floor, this simple and arbitrary act of mine takes on its own conflagrant life. I understand now how the myth of Christ took root!

A BOLD AND BLATANT LIE
WHICH GENIUS HAS CONCEIVED.
THE MORE FAR-FETCHED THE LIE
THE MORE THAT IT'S BELIEVED.
TENS BY TENS
THEY GATHER.
SUCKERS IN THE PARK.
DOZENS BY THE DOZENS MASS
AS GLORYDAY LOOMS
AND THE LIE
BLOOMS!

(He posts a new announcement. The Actress appears and begins to read it. The Actress is young, dressed casually. She wears dark shades.)

46

PRIEST and THE ACTRESS.
  "IN TWO WEEKS
  ON TUESDAY
  AT ONE P.M. SHARP
  A MIRACLE WILL OCCUR
  WITNESS TO THE FAITH
  YOU'LL FIND SALVATION HERE;
  FROM THE DEPTHS OF THE POND
  CHRIST WILL APPEAR!
  BELIEVE!
  AND BE FREE!"
ACTRESS.
  "BELIEVE AND BE FREE … "
Hi.
PRIEST. Hello.
ACTRESS. Nice collar.
PRIEST. Nice sunglasses.
ACTRESS. You're a …
PRIEST. A priest … I bet you're not a priest —
ACTRESS. No … An actress. Was. Still am, technically. Deanna. Me. You read
this?
PRIEST. This?
ACTRESS. This thing. This crazy thing. It's wild.
PRIEST. Wild.
ACTRESS. Fucking wild. Excuse my language. I mean … is it actually possible?
— people were talking — I heard these people talking — that it was actually pos-
sible — and that's just so … fucking wild — and I'm originally from California
so I've seen a lot of wild shit and done a lot of weird, wild shit, but … I don't
know. This. Is it possible?
PRIEST. I think if you have faith, enough faith, anything that seems impossible
becomes possible.
ACTRESS. Oh! *(Suddenly, she throws herself into the Priest's arms — startling him.
She gives a sob. She pulls away. Removes her glasses. She looks into his face then sud-
denly kisses him, deeply and passionately. He enjoys it. She pushes him away.)* Aw-ow.
You're a priest.
PRIEST. I'm a guy.
ACTRESS. Whoops. I didn't mean to do that. Big whoops. It's … you wanna fuck?
PRIEST. *(Aside.)* And so we … fuck. I'm not sure if I know how to … fuck, but
I figure it out, and afterwards I'm in bliss. Bliss. Bliss! I realize that I've denied

myself bliss all these years — and for what?

ACTRESS. Oh Jesus … Not "Jesus" literally … sorry … Well, I've just despoiled a priest. I'm bad. I don't mean to be … it's something that just happens and I've been struggling my whole fucking life and now … I'm despoiling priests. In parks. Behind bushes.

PRIEST. And you do it very well.

ACTRESS. And … is it possible?

PRIEST. You're beautiful.

ACTRESS. Yeah. Is it possible this thing — what they're calling —

PRIEST. The Gloryday.

ACTRESS. That. Is it possible?

PRIEST. Why is it so important to you?

ACTRESS.

I HAD JUST FINISHED SHOOTING
A COFFEE COMMERCIAL,
NATIONAL SPOT
AND RESIDUAL HEAVEN.
MY BOYFRIEND'S ON TV,
A SOAP OPERA VILLAIN.
WE BOTH LIVE IN SPLENDOR
IN BEVERLY HILLS.
THE HILLS THE HILLS THE HILLS …

LIFE COULD NOT HAVE BEEN SWEETER,
I LOVE CALIFORNIA.
WE CELEBRATE SWEEPS MONTH;
COCAINE AND VODKA.
DRIVE THROUGH THE MOUNTAINS,
LAUGHING AND SPEEDING;
THE STARS ARE SO DAZZLING
THE ROAD SPINS AND WEAVES.
OUR CONVERTIBLE JAGUAR
LEAPS OFF THE MOUNTAIN;
THANK GOD I'M TOO STONED
TO BE WEARING MY SEATBELT.
I CRASH AND I TUMBLE
THROUGH CACTUS AND SAGE,
BREAKING MY ARM AND MY NOSE
AND MY JAW AND MY NECK.

OUCH, RIGHT?
SO I WAKE UP IN SURGERY
TEN HOURS LATER.
MY AGENT SENDS FLOWERS.
MY BOYFRIEND IS MISSING.
MY FACE IS DISFIGURED,
IT'S PERFECTLY RUINED.
THE STAR TAKES MY PICTURE
I'M NEWS FOR A WEEK.
THEN THE AGENCY CANCELS
MY COFFEE COMMERCIAL.
IT'S FAREWELL, GOODBYE
TO RESIDUAL HEAVEN.
THANK GOD FOR THE MORPHINE,
THANK GOD FOR MY DEALER,
AND FOR THE VODKA
THAT MELLOWS THE COKE.
THE COKE. THE COKE. THE COKE. THE COKE. THE COKE.
THE COKE.

YEAH.

I COULD USE A LITTLE HELP.
I COULD USE A LITTLE HOPE.
I COULD USE A LITTLE SOMETHING THAT HAS WORTH
AND ILLUMINATES THE POINT
OF MY BEING ON THIS EARTH.
LOOK — I LOOK AROUND THE EARTH
AND I SEE
I DON'T NEED AN AGENT.
I DON'T NEED A JOB.
I DON'T NEED THE COKE OR BOOZE.
I CAN KICK 'EM IF I CHOOSE.
BUT I COULD USE
A LITTLE MIRACLE.
YEAH.
I COULD USE
A LITTLE MIRACLE …

I HAD JUST FINISHED SHOOTING
A COFFEE COMMERCIAL
AND AIN'T IT IRONIC?
I DON'T DRINK COFFEE.
COFFEE. COFFEE. COFFEE. COFFEE.
COFFEE. COFFEE. COFFEE.

(She exits.)

PRIEST. I realize that there are others, now, others who are more quietly suc-
cumbing to the joke. *(His Aunt appears. She speaks on the phone with the priest.)*

AUNT. What's all that commotion going on in the park? I seen it all over the
TV. It's interrupting all my stories …

PRIEST. How are you feeling, Aunt Monie?

AUNT. I'm dying. What's all that commotion in the park?

PRIEST. There will be a miracle — or so everyone believes.

AUNT. Ah, somebody started a joke. And everybody believes it now. Bet
someone's making money off of it — like these TV preachers and doctors and
psychics scamming those poor idiots. I wish that *Bonanza* show was still on.
That was a good show.

PRIEST. What does your doctor say?

AUNT. He says I'm dying so I'm dying. What's the big deal?

PRIEST. You're the only family I've got, Aunt Monie — that's the big deal.

AUNT. Oh you. You were always so sentimental. When you gonna toughen up?
Oh — that reporter is on — the sexy one — he's in the park. Now that is one
sexy man. *(She vanishes. The Reporter appears, taping before a camera.)*

REPORTER. As you can see, Carol, there is a crowd gathered here at the pond
— by all accounts, it's a peaceful gathering, though police have been seen patrolling
the area. One can't call it a demonstration but — what? Yes … again? Four. Three
… As you can see, Carol, there is a crowd gathered here at the pond …

PRIEST.

YOU'VE GOT YOUR CRAZIES
FOR JESUS' SAKE
THE LOSERS WHO'VE GOT NOTHING TO LOSE.
YOU'VE GOT YOUR HERDS
OF BROKEN SOULS,
EMOTIONALLY DRAINED BLACK HOLES;
YOU'VE GOT 'EM ALL HERE:
WAITING FOR THE GLORYDAY.

REPORTER. Father, we'd like to ask you for your opinion about this, uh, strange
gathering — is this some sort of mass hysteria or an actual symbol of faith?

PRIEST. Faith. Yes. We need faith more than ever now and this act of devotion
— this gathering of the faithful is a beautiful gesture of our humanity, as well as
a symbol of our eternal hope: We all want to be included in and celebrate the
love of God's heart.

REPORTER. Wait — Father, sorry, can we take that again? Four. Three …

PRIEST.

    YOU'VE GOT YOUR CRIPPLED
    AND BLIND AND DEAF;
    A SELECTION OF AFFLICTIONS
    TO CHOOSE.
    YOU'VE GOT YOUR SHREDS
    OF DESPERATE LIVES;
    YOUR CRIMINALS AND BATTERED WIVES
    ALL GATHERING HERE:
    WAITING FOR THE GLORYDAY.

ACTRESS, AUNT, REPORTER and CPA.

    GLORYDAY
    GLORYDAY
    GLORYDAY
    GLORY — !

PRIEST.

    MOVE OVER GRACELAND
    BYE, BYE LOURDES.
    THE WORLD HAS A NEW RELIGIOUS SHRINE.
    THE POOR AND THE WEALTHY
    ARE COMING IN HORDES.
    BRING YOUR SINS
    AND FORM A LINE

(A flurry of excitement has burst out in anticipation of the Gloryday.)

    FOR THE

ALL.

    T-SHIRTS!

PRIEST.

    FUNNY HATS!
    PAMPHLETS!

PRIEST and ACTRESS.

    POSTER ART!

ALL.

    T-SHIRTS!

PRIEST and AUNT.
    STATUETTES!
PRIEST and CPA.
    PRAYER BOOKS!
PRIEST and REPORTER.
    TOURING MAPS!
ALL.
    T-SHIRTS!
PRIEST, REPORTER and CPA.
    GLORYDAY!
ACTRESS, AUNT and CPA.
    GLORYDAY!
AUNT and CPA.
    GLORYDAY!
    GLORYDAY!
ACTRESS, AUNT, REPORTER and CPA.
    GLORYDAY!

PRIEST.	**COMPANY.**
"IN THREE DAYS	
	IN THREE DAYS
ON TUESDAY	
	ON TUESDAY
AT ONE P.M. SHARP	
	A MIRACLE — "
A MIRACLE	
WILL OCCUR.	
DO NOT EMBRACE THE LIES	*LIES*
OR THE DOUBTS BELIEVED BY SOME — "	

COMPANY.
    "FROM THE DEPTHS OF THE POND
    OUR LORD SHALL COME!"
ALL.
    GLORYDAY!
    GLORYDAY!
    GLORYDAY!
    GLORYDAY!
    GLORYDAY!
    GLORYDAY!
    GLORYDAY!

GLORYDAY!
PRIEST.
YOU'VE GOT YOUR CRAZIES
FOR JESUS' SAKE
THE LOSERS WHO'VE GOT
NOTHING TO LOSE —
COMPANY.
GLORY!
PRIEST.
YOU'VE GOT YOUR CRIPPLED
AND BLIND AND DEAF;
A SELECTION OF AFFLICTIONS
TO CHOOSE —
COMPANY.
GLORYDAY!
PRIEST.
AND VULNERABILITY TO USE
AS WE WAIT …
COMPANY.
AS WE WAIT …

PRIEST.	**COMPANY.**
FOR THE GLORYDAY!	DAY
	ACTRESS/AUNT.
	GLORYDAY!
GLORY!	
	REPORTER/CPA.
	GLORYDAY!
GLORY!	
	ACTRESS/AUNT.
	GLORYDAY!
GLORY!	
	REPORTER/CPA.
	GLORYDAY!

ACTRESS and AUNT.
GLORY!
ALL.
GLORY!
GLORY
DAY!

(The park explodes with festivities. The Priest wanders away and find himself in a bar. The Reporter is there, off duty, getting tidily drunk.)

REPORTER. Hey, Father! Whatcha drinkin'?

PRIEST. Gin and tonic.

REPORTER. — So be it! You know I've gotta say: I envy you. I really do. I wish I were you — not a priest necessarily, but you know.

PRIEST. I know.

REPORTER. I mean you probably have a better handle on this whole circus — I don't. This is the shittiest assignment I've had since — I hate it. People are actually serious about this — Like — how to get an angle on how anyone can have faith in a time and place where fucking humanity — I mean — what humanity? Look around. What humanity?

PRIEST. What humanity, sure.

REPORTER. It's a shitty assignment, you know?

PRIEST. I know.

REPORTER. Yeah, and you're talking to a guy who loves what he does, who's always wanted to do what I do, no joke, and boy did it piss my dad off, but I always wanted to — "Reporter Extraordinario!" — I was born for the camera! Yeah. Look: I'm just saying. I envy you. I can't go in and videotape people's fucking souls.

PRIEST. No, you can't.

REPORTER. You're right, I can't.

PRIEST. So be it.

REPORTER. You know, Father, we've met before.

PRIEST. That so? When?

REPORTER. Last year. Last year, during the "Tragedy" — you know, "America's Tragedy." Whatever we were calling it — I was downtown covering the fucking disaster — I remember bumping into you — you were running toward. I was running away.

PRIEST. I don't remember.

REPORTER. I do.

    CURIOSITY
    MADE ME LOOK OUT OF THE WINDOW
    ON A BRIGHT BLUE CRISP BLUE DAY.
    CURIOSITY
    MADE ME STARE INTO THE FIRE
    THAT WAS COMING RIGHT MY WAY.
    CURIOSITY
    MADE ME WONDER WHAT WOULD HAPPEN
    IF I CHOSE TO WATCH AND STAY.

BUT INSTINCT MADE ME RUN,
LEAVING FRIENDS AND EVERYONE
TO THE FIRE
COMING OUR WAY —

YOU'RE LOOKING FOR ANSWERS.
SO AM I.
THAT'S WHAT PEOPLE DO.
THE INSTINCT TO WONDER IS HUMAN.
THE INSTINCT TO SURVIVE IS, TOO.

CURIOSITY
ALMOST ENDED MY EXISTENCE
ON A BRIGHT BLUE, CRISP BLUE DAY;
BUT NOW I BURN
WITH THE NEED TO LEARN
THE REASON HUMANS PRAY ...

(The bar vanishes. The Priest returns to the park.)
ACTRESS and CPA.
PLEASE FORGIVE US, FATHER
PLEASE FORGIVE OUR SIN.
ACTRESS, CPA and REPORTER.
HELP US FIX WHAT'S BROKEN
FROM WITHIN.
PRIEST. *(Over the prayer.)* It's impossible not to admire my handicraft: this enormous work of fiction I've created. And I don't feel guilt. Absolutely no guilt. I don't feel ... I don't feel anything, it's as though I am outside of my body and I see myself eating and breathing and sleeping and there is no sense of time. This is what it's like to be God, I realize. I only watch and I only listen.
ACTRESS, CPA and REPORTER.
MAKE US WANT FOR HEAVEN.
LEAD US TO BELIEF.
LET THERE BE A BLESSING
FOR OUR GRIEF.
FALLEN ANGELS, ALL OF US,
WITH WINGS UNFIT TO FLY.
YOU CAN HEAL US, FATHER.
MAKE US FIT TO FLY.

IF NOT THAT,
AT LEAST GIVE BACK
OUR REASON
TO TRY …

PRIEST. People would think I was insane if they knew what I've done. I am not insane. Insanity is doing the same thing over and over again and expecting different results. Praying is that.

THE LIE …
THE LIE BECOMES THE TRUTH.
THE TRUTH, THE TRUTH …
THE —

IN ONE HOUR.
ON THIS DAY.
T-SHIRTS.
FUNNY HATS.

It's time!

THE GREATEST PRACTICAL JOKE
PLAYED ON THE COMMON FOLK
IS

God. Aunt Monie would love all the celebrities! *(The atmosphere around him is heated, nervous — thousands of people are gathering.)*

DIANE SAWYER!
JESSE JACKSON!
STEPHEN KING AND
OPRAH WINFREY!
AL PACINO!
OVER THERE — LOOK:
IT'S CHER!

(The CPA enters.)

CPA. Father. I know what you are: You can't fool me, oh no you can't. I'm going to tell my family and friends. I know that you're *an angel* — All that has been lost will be found; and today, my God will see me again! Gloryday is here! *(He exits.)*

PRIEST.

THERE'S PETE HAMILL.
AND MARK HAMILL.
DOROTHY HAMILL.
DONNY OSMOND
AND HIS FAM'LY;

JOINING THEM:
EMINEM!

(The Actress enters.)

ACTRESS. Hey! I've been looking for you! It's me: Deanna! Me! About the
other day, when I — when we, haha — I just wanted to tell you that, oh god,
I've been thinking about you and how nice and decent you were and because I
met you and because you believed that this whole fantastic thing could happen,
well, it moved me. It really really moved me and for the first time in, I don't
know, fucking forever, I am so — what? Hungry. Nonono, not hungry — I
mean. Yeah. Clean. Really really really clean. And actually, hungry, too, blawha-
ha! Thank you! Thank you thank you thank you! *(She kisses him passionately.)*
Ohmagod, it's my agent. Charles! Hey! *(To the Priest.)* Look: I love you. Thank
you. I love you. *(Off.)* Charles! *(To the Priest.)* Thank you. *(Off.)* It's me! Deanna!
Hey! *(To the Priest.)* I love you! *(She exits.)*

PRIEST.

> A SOLEMN VENEER
> BARELY COVERS THEIR PANIC;
> A ROSTER THAT READS
> LIKE A MODERN TITANIC.
> WON'T IT BE FUN
> TO WATCH THEM ALL DROWN?
> THE MIGHTY AND WEAK
> SUCKED IN AND PULLED DOWN —
> THE DALAI LAMA'S LAWYER!
> THE MAYOR'S EX-WIFE!
> MILK-FED CHRISTIANS!
> WORRIED JEWS!
> FRAGILE MUSLIMS!
> HOPEFUL HINDUS!
> DIANE SAWYER!
> JESSE JACKSON!
> TIME
> TO FEED THE LIONS!

REPORTER. Yes, Carol, a hush has fallen over the entire park — in a few short
minutes, the faithful hope to encounter a miracle here — as outrageous as it may
seem, this phenomenon of faith has captured the hearts of the whole world —
the question today is not, "Will a miracle occur", but "Do you believe?" And I
have to say, Carol … I have to say … Nothing. There's nothing to be said …
(The Priest's Aunt appears.)

PRIEST. Aunt Monie — what are you doing here?

AUNT. Why not? Everyone else is. And I heard that Al Pacino was here. I always liked him.

PRIEST. Go home. You're not well.

AUNT. Look at all the flowers! It reminds me of the sixties.

PRIEST. It's all bullshit and you know it.

AUNT. Why are you here? Where is your priest-thing-neck-thing?

PRIEST. I'm here because — I'm observing.

AUNT. Now who's talking bullshit — oh…! *(A pain shoots through her entire body.)*

PRIEST. You need to sit down. *(He leads her to a park bench.)*

AUNT. I'm sick, so what about it? Look around at this crowd of freaks. I fit right in.

PRIEST. Why are you here?

AUNT. To see what happens.

PRIEST. Nothing will happen. You know that. It's a huge, elaborate joke. It's hysteria. You know how people are. You told me how gullible people are — they'll believe in a deliberate lie because they're too frightened of the truth.

AUNT. What is the truth, Michael?

PRIEST. You know what the truth is.

AUNT. No. I don't. Not anymore. Maybe, all these years, when I was so sure that God did not exist, I wasn't sure at all. There was always something scratching inside the walls, *capice?* I was lying. I know this. And I feel … so sad.

PRIEST. Aunt Monie. Listen to me: It's a joke, all of this. I know who did it. I know the perpetrator. And I know that the whole point of this joke was to show all these poor idiots that God is no more!

AUNT. What are you saying? What are you saying, Michael?

PRIEST. God is … no more. I believe God is no more.

AUNT. But … I love you. Where does that come from? It has to come from somewhere; not just from me … it has to come from somewhere bigger than our instincts. It has to come from —

PRIEST. — Let's go home.

AUNT.
> THERE WILL BE A MIRACLE.
> STICK AROUND AND SEE.
> YOU NEED PATIENCE FOR A MIRACLE.
> TIMING IS THE KEY.
> COULD NOT HAVE HAPPENED YESTERDAY.
> AND TOMORROW IS TOO LATE.
> THE MOMENT HAS TO BE EXACT
> AND UNTIL THEN YOU HAVE TO WAIT.

YOU CAN NEVER RUSH A MIRACLE.
YOU CAN'T FORCE A THING TO BE.
I AM DESPERATE FOR A MIRACLE;
BUT IT WON'T COME JUST FOR ME.
WE WILL ALL SHARE THE MIRACLE.
AS EVERYBODY SHOULD:
LITTLE ONES.
GROCERY CLERKS.
CPAS
MOVIE STARS.
BATTERED WIVES, DYING BOYS,
HUNGRY SOULS, THE WORST OF MEN
ALONG WITH THE GOOD —
I ALWAYS KNEW THERE WOULD BE A MIRACLE;
I'VE WONDERED WHEN AND HOW.
AND I WILL SEE A MIRACLE.
THERE WILL BE A MIRACLE.
IF NOT SOON;
NOW …
(She begins to nod off on her nephew's shoulder.)
THERE WILL BE A MIRACLE.
WE WILL SEE A MIRACLE …
PRIEST. Shhh … Rest …
AUNT.
WAKE ME FOR THE MIRACLE …
WAKE ME FOR THE …
PRIEST. Shhh … *(He kisses his Aunt tenderly and leaves her to rest on the bench. A strangely beautiful, but menacing color fills the park — the air begins to shimmer, like sparkling glass. The vast multitude holds its breath — it's as though the planet itself had stopped rotating; time is stalled.)* Four minutes … Wait … Everyone … Please listen to me …
ACTRESS, CPA and REPORTER.
PLEASE FORGIVE US, FATHER.
PRIEST. You have to go home — this — this is a joke! A terrible, terrible joke!
ACTRESS, CPA and REPORTER.
PLEASE FORGIVE OUR SIN.
PRIEST. I know, because — I created it! Hell yes! I created it all! And it's gotten way way way out of hand —

59

ACTRESS, CPA and REPORTER.
  HELP US FIX WHAT'S BROKEN
  FROM WITHIN.
PRIEST. Two minutes! Nothing will happen! Listen to me! It was a trick — I wanted — I wasn't meaning to hurt anyone —
ACTRESS, CPA and REPORTER.
  FALLEN ANGELS, ALL OF US
PRIEST. Go home! All of you!
ACTRESS, CPA and REPORTER.
  WITH WINGS UNFIT TO FLY
PRIEST. I'm sorry! You hear? I'm sorry!
ACTRESS, CPA and REPORTER.
  YOU CAN HEAL US FATHER
PRIEST. *(Breaking down)* I was only trying to … I'm so sorry …
ACTRESS, CPA and REPORTER.
  MAKE US FIT TO —
(A tremendous explosion of thunder shakes the park — a stab of lightning momentarily blinds the Priest. There's a sense of time standing still.)
CPA.
  THE SKY GOES GREY
  THEN TURNS INTO BLACKNESS
  ERASING DAY.
AUNT and CPA.
  A WIND BEGINS
  AND BUILDS TO THE HOWL
  OF A MILLION SINS.
ACTRESS, CPA and REPORTER.
  A LIGHTNING FLASH
  THEN MORE, AND THE CLOUDS
  WRITHE WITH EVERY SLASH.
ACTRESS, CPA, REPORTER and ACTRESS.
  A MIST APPEARS
  AND HANGS IN THE AIR
  LIKE A SPIDER'S TEARS.

  A VIOLENT SHAKE
  AND A CHURNING TWISTER
  CONSUMES THE LAKE.

THE RAIN POURS HARD
AS THE CYCLONE GROWS
AND THE LEAVES ARE RIPPED OFF
THE CRACKING BRANCHES
SCREAMS AND SHOUTS
AND THE FLIGHT OF MASSES
SPINNING, MANIC,
BURSTING, GLOWING
GLOWING, GLOWING — !

PRIEST.
EVERYONE FLEES
WITHOUT LOOKING BACKWARDS.
EVERYONE FLEES.

BUT I LOOK BACK
TO THE SWIRLING TWISTER
I LOOK BACK.

AND I SEE
WHAT NOBODY SEES
AND I SEE

RISING UP
FROM THE DEPTHS OF THE POND
RISING UP:

GLORY!
GLORY!
GLORY …

(A wave of wonder washes over his face. His eyes follow a sight too wondrous to behold as it sails up from the pond, up into the air, up into the sky. After a moment, his Aunt appears.)

AUNT. Michael — are you okay?

PRIEST. Aunt Monie — did you see…?

AUNT. I got soaked — you got soaked. Look at us …

PRIEST. Did you see — from the pond! Aunt Monie —

AUNT. I couldn't see anything, honey. What happened?

PRIEST. You didn't — ?

AUNT. I guess I fell asleep, and then it started raining and that woke me up and

all I saw was everyone running and it was so dark … So. *(The Reporter straggles in.)*
PRIEST. You — hey! Did you see it happen?!
REPORTER. You gotta be kidding — I was running for cover — Christ, what a complete bust. *(He exits.)*
PRIEST. No — it happened — wait! *(The Actress hurries by.)* Hey! Deanna! *(He runs and hugs her joyfully.)* Did you see! It happened!!!
ACTRESS. *(Pushing him away, brusquely.)* Get off — god.
PRIEST. You saw what happened — didn't you?
ACTRESS. No. I saw nothing. Nothing. Nothing … *(She puts her sunglasses on and stumbles away.)*
PRIEST. A miracle! It was a miracle! I saw…! *(The CPA enters. Naked.)* You — you saw it, didn't you!!! *(The CPA stops, grabs the priest violently — then drops him, in hopelessness. He exits.)* Aunt Monie — I saw — didn't anyone see? Did anyone see? ANYONE?!
AUNT. Settle down. Let's go home. We'll get something to eat —
PRIEST. A miracle. I saw, Aunt Monie … You believe me, don't you?
AUNT. If you say so, baby. Why not? *(She pats his face and exits.)*
PRIEST.
> WHY NOT…?
> I GUESS …
> I THINK …
> WHY NOT …

A month later, at Aunt Monica's funeral, I put on the collar again … but … I'm not celebrating Mass. Not yet … I'm … because … I created a lie that became the truth. The lie was for everyone. But the truth was only for myself. So what do I do with it? Monsignor? What do I do with the truth?
> I SAW …
> I FELT …
> LAST YEAR …
> AND NOW …
> WHAT NOW …

PRIEST and COMPANY.
> THE TRUTH
> THE TRUTH
> THE TRUTH
> THE TRUTH …

(Lights.)

End of Play

PROPERTY LIST

Knife
Red scarf
Martinis
Electrical wire
Stiletto knife
Paper, pen
Phone
Microphone, camera
Drinks

SOUND EFFECTS

Thunder